Ardelean Gheorghe Cornel (BIGAGC)

MEDITATIONS
VOL.48

NARCOSIA Publishing -2008

Reading and applying these, quotes, ideas
1) You save time, self-training and accumulatea lot of useful information immediately.
2) You manage to achieve your personal goals much faster, more efficiently.
3) You manage to prevent many unpleasant surprises, mistakes, failures, problems, illnesses, etc.
4) You manage to become more optimistic, more positive, more creative, more adaptable, more flexible, more efficient, more confident in yourself, more constructive, etc.

ABOUT ME

Rachel Mitchell AutorProducer TV/Film/ Documentaries – Director of Programming & Investor BUILTinAMERICA.tv
I appreciate every thing you wrote Ardelean Gheorghe Cornel (BIGAGC)you are a wealth of wisdom

Ardelean Gheorghe Cornel (BIGAGC)

MEDITATIONS
VOL.48

NARCOSIA Publishing
ARAD COUNTY, MACEA
2008

CIP description of the Romanian National Library

Ardelean Gheorghe Cornel (BIGAGC)

ISBN 978-606-8048-27-7

Urge to read, analyze and apply these meditations

By reading and analyzing the meditations of (BIGAGC) by applying one or more thoughts we will find solutions that will help us:

I. Discover:
1. qualities;
2. defects;
3. capabilities;
4. skills;
5. some opportunities
to succeed in life;
6. finding a partner for life;
7. keeping our marriage;
8. discovering our feelings;
9. discovering our mistakes;
10. etc..

II. To prevent some:
1. mistakes;
2. accidents;
3. divorces;
4. trouble;
5. bankruptcies;
6. failures;
7. conflicts;
8. etc..

III. Become:
1. more efficient;
2. happier;
3. more loved;
4. more honorable;
5. appreciated;
6. more respected;
7. more loved;
8. more organized;

9. more optimistic;
10. more plan;
11. most active;
12. best;
13. fairer;
14. more humane;
15. more unselfish;
16. popular;
17. more famous;
18. etc..

IV. Come out of:
1. the state of lost hope;
2. the state of pessimism;
3. the state of despair;
4. the state of passivity;
5. the state of inactivity
6. etc..

V. Participate at:

1. social life;
2. political life;
3. the activity of non-profit organization
4. etc..

VI. Find more opportunities to meet favorable or more favorable conditions.

VII. To let us change our lives more in better, to make it more beautiful.

VIII. To expand our chances to find the right partner for life.

IX. To let us realize and to

maintain a happy marriage.

X. To let us raise and educate our children better, to take more care of them.

I am writing these meditations and adding these books, other publications and on the Internet, etc.. because we need them every day and it is necessary to apply them so that we each achieve what we want: a more beautiful life, a more prosperous and happy one. These meditations reflect a tiny part of reality, of what would be good to be present in real life and in human relations.

I expect good news from you, good deeds that you have done influenced by the fact that you have read and applied one or more ideas to make your life more beautiful, more prosperous, more happy and to be positive lively models for others.

Each of us can become a positive new model for those around us thus participating in the creation of a better human society, of a more prosperous one, and a happier one.

I would be very happy and excited if one or more ideas that you have read, help you in one way or another or make you happier, more prosperous, etc..

I wish you all health, happiness and the achieving of all things that you want.

I expect your news, ideas, opinions, troubles and joys, etc..

Sincerely, love and with much joy,
    I invite you to visit my site http://www.bigagc.com and to write to me at: aradforex@gmail.com

"Ardelean Gheorghe Cornel"
(BIGAGC)

VOLUME 48

1)   A positive conception of life creates more chances of finding the right partner for life.

2)   A positive conception of life helps us become more credible.

3)   The uncertainties of incomes discourage people.

4)   The uncertainties of incomes form the development of insecurity.

5)   The uncertainties of incomes make it hard to become more credible.

6)   Those who discover unique ways to work efficiently for a better life are creative people.

7)   Those who discover unique ways to work efficiently for a better life have the possibility to maintain a happy marriage.

8)   Those who discover unique ways to

work efficiently for a better life have more and greater chances to meet more favorable situations.

9)   Those who know how to take advantage of the opportunity of creation have more chances to maintain efficient co operations.

10)   Those who know how to take advantage of the opportunity of creation increase their chances of achieving a mature love.

11)   Those who control circumstances have a greater ability to prevent many failures.

12)   Those who control circumstances must be rewarded.

13)   Those who control circumstances increase their credibility.

14)   Those who know that discipline is the key of dreams have the ability to maintain their desired efficient co

operations.

15) Those who know that discipline is one of the symbolic keys have a greater ability to maintain their mature love.

16) Those who know that discipline is one of the symbolic keys have a greater capacity to achieve a more beautiful life.

17) Those who have had better economical and social conditions during their evolution must be appreciated.

18) Those who have had better economical and social conditions during their evolution have a greater ability to meet more favorable situations.

19) Those who have had better economical and social conditions during their evolution have a greater ability to achieve more outstanding performances.

20) Those who passionately live their life have more chances to maintain their desired social relations.

21)   Those who live life passionately have a greater ability to achieve a more beautiful life.

22)   Those who have opportunities to develop have more chances to succeed.

23)   Those who have opportunities to develop have more and greater chances to achieve more outstanding performances.

24)   Those who willingly expand their experience have more chances to achieve their desired future.

25)   Those who willingly expand their positive experience must be supported.

26)   The need to succeed maintains the chances of achieving our own happiness.

27)   The need to succeed contributes a lot in maintaining efficient co operations.

28)   Most of those who wander without purpose in life have smaller chances of success.

29)   Most of those who wander without

a purpose in life maintain their social relations a lot harder.

30)   Most of those who wander without a purpose in life have fewer chances of becoming more efficient.

31)   The ability to consciously choose is an engine of development in all areas of activity.

32)   A positive enterprising spirit increases our possibility of maintaining the desired social relations.

33)   A positive enterprising spirit increases our ability of achieving efficient global important co operations.

34)   Efficient people in positive actions have greater chances of achieving their desired future.

35)   Efficient people in positive actions have more chances of succeeding in life.

36)   Efficient people in positive actions have more chances to achieve efficient co-

developments.

37) Efficient people in positive actions have more chances of maintaining the desired effective co-developments.

38) The sense of quality must be appreciated.

39) The sense of quality increases our ability to achieve valuable products.

40) Constructive thinking is a necessity.

41) Constructive thinking increases our credibility.

42) Constructive thinking helps us make fewer mistakes.

43) People who respect themselves also have a humanist behavior.

44) People who respect themselves are engines of development in all areas of activity.

45) Most of those involved in several projects must be rewarded.

46) The majority of those involved in

many projects increase their efficiency a lot faster.

47)   People who control their emotions must be supported.

48)   People who control their emotions have greater chances to achieve true friendships.

49)   Problems are solved through positive methods.

50)   Those who are remarkably gifted mostly have a positive thinking.

51)   Those who are remarkably gifted mostly have the sense of discipline.

52)   Those who are remarkably gifted are mostly balanced.

53)   Those who are remarkably gifted have a continuous care for good health.

54)   Successful people have a great ability to cope with mental stress.

55)   Successful people mostly have the ability to improvise when needed.

56) People who have successes most of the times have high goals in life.
57) People who have successes also have a positive conception of life.
58) People who have successes also have a positive self image.
59) People who have successes mostly have their own value system.
60) People who have successes are mostly efficient.
61) People who have successes are mostly responsible.
62) People who have successes are mostly communicative.
63) People who have successes are mostly energetic.
64) People who have successes mostly understand when it is necessary for them to be so.
65) People who have successes are mostly ready to help others when they

have the possibility to help them.

66) Long term thinking must be promoted.

67) Long term thinking increases our credibility.

68) Long term thinking creates the possibility to become more efficient.

69) Long term thinking creates better conditions to achieve more outstanding performances.

70) Long term thinking contributes a lot to achieving a very beautiful life.

71) Those who have high objectives in life mostly have a creative thinking.

72) Those who have high objectives in life also have the sense of organization.

73) Those who have high objectives in life are cooperative in activities.

74) Those who have high objectives in life mostly trust others.

75) Those who have high objectives in

life are mostly reliable people.
76)   Those who have high objectives in life are mostly emotionally stable.
77)   Those who have high objectives in life mostly do not have prejudices.
78)   Those who have high objectives in life are mostly objective.
79)   Those who have high objectives in life are mostly oriented towards the outside world.
80)   Those who have high objectives in life are mostly oriented towards their task.
81)   Those who have high objectives in life are mostly careful with others.
82)   Those who have high objectives in life mostly have a very real image of themselves.
83)   Those who have high objectives in life are mostly full of energy.
84)   Those who have high objectives in life are mostly people who are used to

carry out the activities they have started.

85)   The sense of achieving quality in everything we do helps us a lot not to make any more mistakes.

86)   The sense of achieving quality in everything we do imposes us to use a realistic thinking.

87)   The sense of achieving quality in everything we do must be promoted.

88)   The sense of achieving quality in everything we do helps us maintain a happy marriage.

89)   The sense of achieving quality in everything we do helps us a lot to prevent almost all the possible failures and even all of them because it is not impossible.

90)   People who have the ability to take rapid quality decisions also have a constructive thinking.

91)   People who have the ability to take rapid quality decisions must be supported.

92) People who have the ability to take rapid quality decisions continuously perfect themselves.

93) People who have the ability to take rapid quality decisions are engines of development in all areas of activity.

94) People who have the ability to take rapid quality decisions have great chances to achieve their desired future

95) People who have the ability to take rapid quality decisions have many creative qualities.

96) Persons with human social behaviors must also have a positive thinking.

97) People with human social behaviors need to have the sense of fairness.

98) Persons with human social behaviors have more qualities to achieve efficient global co operations.

99) People with human social behaviors

trust themselves.

100) Persons with human social behaviors have more chances to find the right partner for life.

101) People with human social behaviors have more chances to become even more efficient.

102) Those who do not have hopes, in order to create hopes for the future they need to act to respect rights.

103) Those who do not have hopes, in order to create hopes for the future they need to form and develop their long term thinking.

104) Those who do not have hopes, in order to create hopes for the future they need to connect with those who know how to find favorable situations.

105) Those who do not have hopes, in order to create hopes for the future they need to connect with those who have an

efficient thinking.

106) Those who do not have hopes, in order to create hopes for the future they need to connect with those people who solve problems through positive methods.

107) Those who do not have hopes, in order to create hopes for the future they need to connect with people with preventive thinking.

108) Those who do not have hopes, in order to create hopes for the future they need to connect with people who have a constructive conception of life.

109) Those who do not have hopes, in order to create hopes for the future they need to connect with people who have a global thinking.

110) Those who do not have hopes, in order to create hopes for the future they need to connect the people who also have the sense of equity.

111) Those who do not have hopes, in order to create hopes for the future they need to connect with people who have succeeded in being happy in their life.

112) Persons who do not have hopes, in order to create hopes for the future they need to connect with people who also have the sense of responsibility.

113) People who do not have hopes, in order to create hopes for the future they need to connect with people who have succeeded in maintaining a mature love.

114) People who do not have hopes, in order to create hopes for the future they need to connect with people who have succeeded to become credible from predictable.

115) Persons who do not have hopes, in order to create hopes for the future they need to connect with people who have the ability to take rapid decisions.

116) People who have been in prison rightfully or wrongfully, and after being released they have succeeded, they must become living models for every person no matter what their status is, either head of state or a person in prison.

117) People who have not succeeded in achieving a happy marriage up to a certain date need to keep their hope of a happy marriage.

118) Most of those who have not succeeded in making a happy marriage up to a certain date, in order to succeed they need to form and develop their positive enterprising spirit.

119) Those who have not succeeded in making a happy marriage up to a certain date, in order to succeed they need to form and develop an anticipative thinking.

120) People who have not succeeded in forming a happy marriage up to a certain

date, in order to succeed they need to form and develop a great ability to find their desired partner for life.

121) People who have not succeeded in making a happy marriage up to a certain date, in order to succeed they need to form and develop the ability of making positive changes that are mandatory in their professional life.

122) Most of those who have not succeeded in making a happy marriage up to a certain date, in order to succeed they need to form and develop the ability to choose the road that fits them best.

123) People who have not succeeded in making a happy marriage up to a certain date, in order to succeed they need to form and develop the ability to follow their calling.

124) All of those who have not succeeded in making a happy marriage up

to a certain date, in order to succeed they need to form and develop the ability to form and develop a constructive conception of life.

125) People who have not succeeded in making a happy marriage up to a certain date, in order to succeed they need to form and develop the ability of making and maintaining true friendships easily.

126) Persons who have not succeeded in making a happy marriage up to a certain date, in order to succeed they need to form and develop the ability to find new solutions in achieving and maintaining a happy marriage.

127) People who have not succeeded in making a happy marriage up to a certain date, in order to succeed they need to form and develop the ability to achieve, develop and maintain their own happiness.

128) Most of those who have not

succeeded in making a happy marriage up to a certain date, in order to succeed they need to form and develop more and greater chances to meet more favorable situations.

129) Those who have not succeeded in making a happy marriage up to a certain date, in order to succeed they need to form and develop the ability to identify and replace inefficient ideas with more efficient ones.

130) All of those who have not succeeded in making a happy marriage up to a certain date, in order to succeed they need to form and develop the ability to form and develop a positive spirit.

131) The ability to form, develop and maintain only positive behaviors must be promoted.

132) The ability to form, develop and maintain only positive behaviors helps a

lot in achieving the desired future.

133) The ability to form, develop and maintain only positive behaviors contributes a lot to maintaining a mature love.

134) The ability to form, develop and maintain only positive behaviors keeps the ability to obtain more and greater outstanding performances.

135) People who know how to take quality decisions also have the sense of achievement.

136) People who know how to take quality decisions have more chances to achieve their desired future.

137) Persons who know how to take quality decisions have more chances of becoming even more efficient.

138) All of those who know how to take quality decisions also develop their sense of efficiency.

139) Persons who know how to take quality decisions develop their sense of planning.

140) People who know how to take quality decisions develop their sense of self control.

141) A great capacity of continuous self perfection helps us maintain our humanity.

142) Will helps us become patient.

143) We can contribute to the achievement of our greatest accomplishments also through the contribution of the formation, development, maintenance and usage of imaginative behavior.

144) A great capacity of using available knowledge helps us achieve more efficient co operations.

145) We can overcome the difficulties that we must overcome also through the help of the formation, development,

maintenance and usage of working behavior.

146) A great capacity of maintaining self confidence helps us maintain our humanity.

147) In order to rise up once again for the first time for the who knows what time it is necessary to also form, develop, maintain and use intellectual behavior.

148) Continuously making ourselves efficient helps us become reserved.

149) The necessary qualities in achieving personal goals can be formed, developed, maintained and used also through the contribution of the formation, development, maintenance and usage of voluble behavior.

150) A great capacity of positively influencing people helps us achieve more performances.

151) Creativity helps us become self

controlled.

152) In order to prevent not achieving our personal goals, it is necessary to also form, develop, maintain and use our mannered behavior.

153) A great capacity of encouraging people helps us become more optimistic.

154) A great capacity of remaining involved in the same area with even greater objectives must be encouraged.

155) A great capacity of working hard helps us become more preventive.

156) In order to escape poverty it is necessary to also form, develop, maintain and use friendly behavior.

157) A great capacity of being oneself helps us achieve more favorable situations.

158) A great capacity of more efficiently using financial means helps us achieve more pleasant surprises.

159) Obtaining more and greater successes can be achieved also through the contribution of the formation, development, maintenance, usage of an intellectual behavior.

160) We can prevent some failures also through the contribution of the formation, development, maintenance and usage of productive behavior.

161) Aspiring towards a more meaningful life can also be achieved through the formation, development, maintenance and usage of continuous self efficient behavior.

162) A great capacity of cherishing oneself helps us become tolerant.

163) A great capacity of establishing even greater personal goals helps us achieve more personal goals.

164) A great capacity of continuous self perfection must be imitated.

165) A great capacity of using a value system helps us achieve more efficient co operations.

166) We can overcome the difficulties that we must overcome also through the help of the formation, development, maintenance and usage of sportive behavior.

167) The radical transformation for the better of our life can be achieved also through the formation, development, maintenance and usage of peacemaking behavior.

168) Continuous self-motivation helps us achieve much more efficient co operations.

169) A great capacity of being friendly helps us become more pleasant.

170) A great capacity of achieving human relationships helps us become more tolerant.

171) We can become stronger and we can not allow ourselves to be influenced by the world also through the contribution of the formation, development, maintenance and usage of balanced behavior.

172) A great capacity of increasing creativity helps us become optimistic.

173) Our happiness depends a lot also on the formation, development, maintenance and usage of self-controlled behavior.

174) The limits of achievement imposed by ourselves in our mind at a given moment can be overcome or eliminated also through the contribution of the formation, development, maintenance and usage of ingenious behavior.

175) A great capacity of persevering until finding creative solutions helps us achieve more efficient co operations.

176) In achieving our successes a

contribution is also brought by the formation, development, maintenance and usage of kind behavior.

177) A great capacity of being creative in order to solve great problems helps us become more loved.

178) A great capacity of more efficiently using time helps us maintain our happiness.

179) A great capacity of enjoying work helps us become more practical.

180) We can form, develop and maintain the state of being ourselves also through the contribution of the formation, development, maintenance and usage of a spiritual behavior.

181) We can contribute to the achievement of our greatest accomplishments also through the contribution of the formation, development, maintenance and usage of

mannered behavior.

182) The radical transformation for the better of our life can be achieved also through the formation, development, maintenance and usage of respectful behavior.

183) A great capacity of using attitudes helps us become understanding.

184) A great capacity of being understanding with people helps us become practical.

185) A great capacity of achieving what was proposed helps us achieve more favorable situations.

186) Problems cannot be solved by the ideas that created them but also through the contribution of the formation, development, maintenance and usage of persistent behavior.

187) Self-imposed discipline helps us become alive.

188) A great capacity of being tolerant with people helps us become optimistic.

189) A great capacity of using each failure to achieve successes helps us become cautious.

190) A great capacity of continuous self perfection must be formed.

191) Continuous self perfection must be appreciated.

192) A great capacity of learning how to achieve personal goals helps us become more efficient.

193) The self efficient use of our time helps us become persevering.

194) A great capacity of continuously positively transforming life helps us become happier.

195) A great capacity of managing life helps us become loving.

196) A great capacity of establishing high personal goals helps us become more

practical.

197) A great capacity of investing efficiently helps us become more enthusiastic.

198) A great capacity of continuously enhancing performances helps us become more practical.

199) Our happiness depends a lot also on the formation, development, maintenance and usage of organized behavior.

200) Continuous self-motivation helps us become efficient.

201) A great capacity of thinking largely helps us maintain our efficiency.

202) A great capacity of establishing even greater personal goals helps us maintain our wisdom.

203) Continuous self-control helps us become cautious.

204) The obstacles that prevent us from achieving our personal goals can be

surpassed also through the contribution of the formation, development, maintenance and usage of audacious behavior.

205) A great capacity of being convincing must be developed.

206) Release from our self-imposed restrictions can be made also through the contribution of the formation, development, maintenance and usage of prejudice-free behavior.

207) Adaptation must be encouraged.

208) Some mistakes can be prevented also through the contribution of the formation, development, maintenance and usage of agreeable behavior.

209) A great capacity of more efficiently using financial means helps us become understanding.

210) The force of our ideas can be augmented also through the contribution of the formation, development,

maintenance and usage of firm behavior.

211) We can contribute to the achievement of our greatest accomplishments also through the contribution of the formation, development, maintenance and usage of idealistic behavior.

212) A great capacity of maintaining self confidence helps us become loving.

213) A great capacity of positively influencing people helps us maintain our way of being liked.

214) The limits of achievement imposed by ourselves in our mind at a given moment can be overcome or eliminated also through the contribution of the formation, development, maintenance and usage of humane behavior.

215) A great capacity of using available ideas helps us become more loved.

216) A great capacity of being honest

with oneself helps us maintain our enthusiasm.

217) A great capacity of being oneself helps us become more humane.

218) Self-imposed discipline helps us become loyal.

219) In order to prevent failures it is necessary to also form, develop, maintain and use self-controlled behavior.

220) A great capacity of creating one's own safety helps us become more understanding.

221) Our happiness depends a lot also on the formation, development, maintenance and usage of peaceful behavior.

222) Pessimism can be removed and replaced with optimism also through the contribution of the formation, development, maintenance and usage of tenacious behavior.

223) Our own happiness can be achieved

and maintained also through the contribution of the formation, development, maintenance and usage of a behavior of being eager for knowledge.

224) In order to rise up once again for the first time for the who knows what time it is necessary to also form, develop, maintain and use hopeful behavior.

225) Cherishing oneself helps us become respectful.

About the author and his ideas

Hmm ... I do not know where to begin. It is difficult to really know someone. Often, the person on whom you stopped is difficult to decipher.

That is not the case of Gheorghe Cornel Ardelean. From the first moment I knew and he got my attention.

I recognized him immediately from the descriptions made by his colleagues: "One small, with white haired man with many books and newspapers in his hand, they said. My curiosity pushed me to address him, cheerful, open; he began to talk to me as if we knew each other for years. A person opened both to dialogue as well as current jokes. I got to know him even better when we met at Club Central. A nice company as long as you succeed not to be attracted in that part of the discussion where his future plans are. Plans that are repeated endlessly become a burden for the people around him. Not because it would be something wrong in what he says but through their very repeatability.

On several occasions I have read some of his meditations, others have been published in the magazine "Freedom in Thought".

By their simplicity and the fact that they expresses absolute truths, for those who do not take seriously the writings of Cornel Gheorghe Ardelean they may seem indeed to read seriously what to write, I bet they will find among the apparently simple lines, a message equal to a person who has suffered enormously because of human and system injustices.

The cry of a man eager for more, eager for simplicity, for the truth and for a Utopia, wishful of a perfect world.

If even 10% of what he writes would be put into practice by us, then certainly we would set ourselves and with others at the same time. Surprisingly, nobody sees that Cornel Gheorghe Ardelean even puts into practice what he writes, which means that he really believes it.

With an analytical style impossible to confuse, Mr. Cornel Gheorghe Ardelean is successful in a few lines and penetrates into the essence of truth. By this thinking, he is venturing into an area still unexplored in specialized literature.

Specialized topics are part of the absolute truths that each of us have deep within our being, so acknowledged, so obvious, so natural that no one has ventured to put them on paper.

But surely there will be many who, after reading and rereading these absolute truths will solve many of the problems of their existence. The novelty that makes Cornel Gheorghe Ardelean stand out besides putting on paper a well-known truth, is that it also leads to problem solving. It is a promising start in an area of astute competition and often an unscrupulous one.

I wish you success Mr. Ardelean and may these meditations help as many people as possible. Do not give up, continue on the path that you have chosen and maybe in the nearer or further future the world will be at least 5% as you want it to be.

Do not give up ... We ... only a few, I must admit, we are beside you.

SIMION SEBASTIAN EDUARD

Graduate of the Academy of Theater and Film
Former journalist of the national newspapers and Romania Libera, Evenimentul Zilei, was Her Majesty's Paul of Romania's adviser
a businessman resident in Italy

I invite you to visit the site: www.bigagc.com

I invite you to join my group on Facbook: (România) GrupPublic

https://www.facebook.com/groups/2283373
91695744/

We invite you to join my Facebook group: (English) GrupPublic

https://www.facebook.com/groups/BIGAGC/

I invite you to join my group on Linkedin:

https://www.linkedin.com/groups/13850051/

I invite you to contact me on Linkedin at

Ardelean Gheorghe Cornel:
linkedin.com/in/gheorghe-cornel-3771971a3

I invite you to write to me by e-mail:
 aradforex@gmail.com

Ardelean Gheorghe Cornel (BIGAGC)

born **03**.11.1954, in Macea, Arad County, Email: aradforex@gmail.com
http://www.bigagc.com/en/books

I have known the economist Cornel Ardelean for dozens of years, as a guy that outraged the thought of some who did not believe in his ideas, innovative, simply put but with a long and efficient duration. After the Revolution he proved that he is indeed a good economist by founding the first small enterprise of Arad County, in the year 1990 of the post-communist age.

I have always been by Cornel Ardelean's side, never ceasing to believe that the man can rise above his time if he wishes to and if he has the potential to do it.

SABIN BODEA
President of the Writers' League of Romania
Arad Branch